STRANGE NATURE

The Insect Portraits of Levon Biss

Words by
GREGORY MONE

Photographs by
LEVON BISS

From the collections of the
OXFORD UNIVERSITY MUSEUM OF NATURAL HISTORY

ABRAMS BOOKS FOR YOUNG READERS

NEW YORK

Cataloging-in-Publication Data has been applied for and
may be obtained from the Library of Congress.

ISBN 978-1-4197-3166-2

Text copyright © 2020 Gregory Mone
Photographs copyright © 2020 Levon Biss
Book design by Heather Kelly

Published in 2020 by Abrams Books for Young Readers, an imprint of ABRAMS.

Printed and bound in China
10 9 8 7 6 5 4 3

ABRAMS The Art of Books
195 Broadway, New York, NY 10007
abramsbooks.com

A huge thanks to Dr. James Hogan, Scott Billings,
and Professor Paul Smith of the Oxford University Museum of
Natural History for their enthusiasm and dedication. Your support and
vision helped make Microsculpture a reality. I will always be grateful.
Big love goes to my family: Isla, Elli & Seb, Leica & Bless, and
of course Thor. Without you nothing is possible.
—L.B.

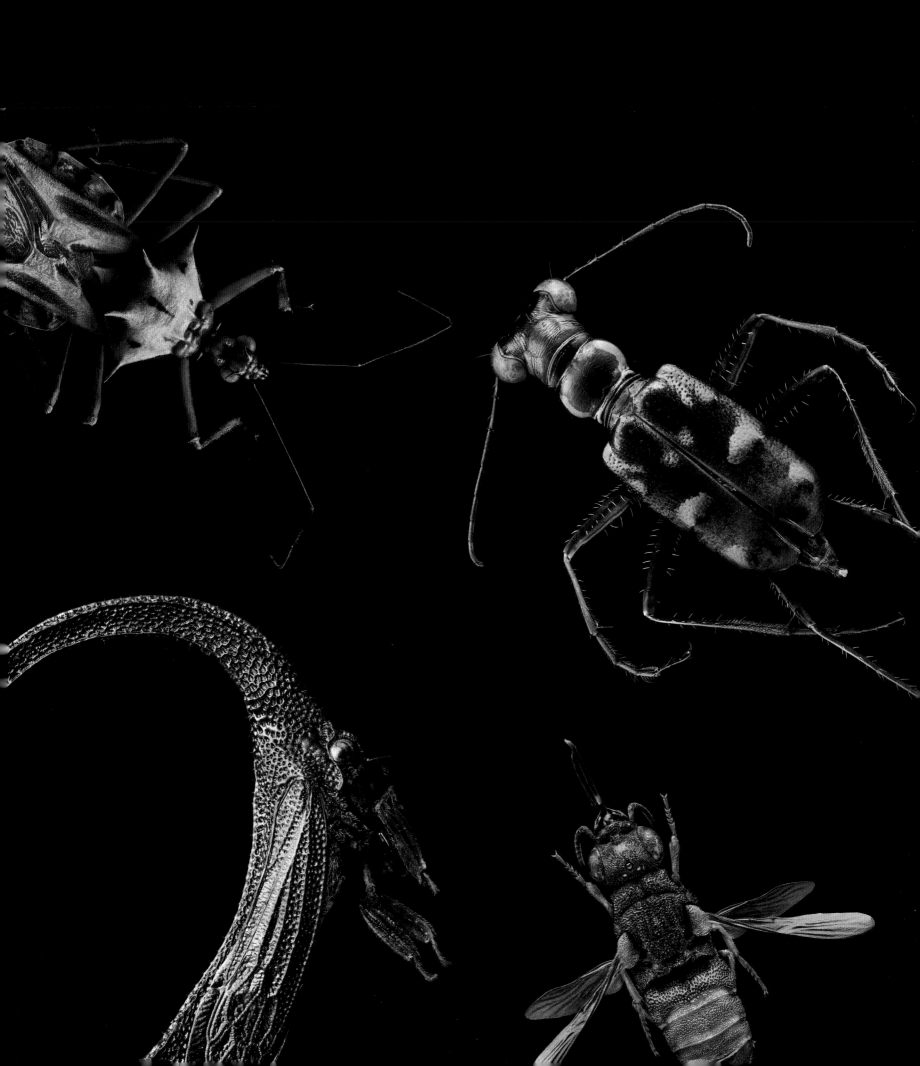

INTRODUCTION

A boy named Sebastian ran into his family's kitchen holding a tiny beetle. Excited, he showed it to his dad, Levon.

The insect wasn't rare or unusual. Sebastian had found it in their backyard. But it really did look strange, so Sebastian and his dad placed it under a microscope to see more.

They were instantly amazed. The two of them quickly learned what the scientists who study insects have known for many, many years. Fantastic miniature monsters walk and creep and crawl and fly all around our planet all the time. We swat at them, stomp on them, or walk right by them without noticing their strange beauty.

Sebastian's dad is a photographer. Normally, he takes pictures of celebrities and presidents and famous sports stars. Bugs? He didn't take pictures of bugs! But he was so amazed by what he saw under the microscope that he wanted anyone to be able to see these fantastic creatures up close. After photographing that first backyard beetle, he selected thirty-seven different insects stored in the famous Oxford University Museum of Natural History to photograph next. Dead ones, obviously. Live bugs don't sit still for portraits.

Levon treated his tiny subjects with the same respect he'd give a world leader or the fastest man alive. And he didn't just take one picture. He used special cameras and lenses and lights to take thousands of photographs of each insect. Finally, he stitched these pictures together on his computer to create an intricate close-up image of each insect.

He called this effort the Microsculpture project.

The images were expanded to ten feet tall or wide, then displayed in museums around the world. In normal life, most of these creatures are so tiny, they could scurry around your pinkie nail, but the Microsculpture project showed what they'd look like if they were as large as a car or a motorcycle. Kids and adults of all ages, all around the world, have stood mesmerized before these giant photos of insects. Now you get to see them for yourself, right here in this book. They're fast, creepy, sneaky, smart, and sometimes a little nasty, and we hope you'll never look at the insects in your backyard the same way again.

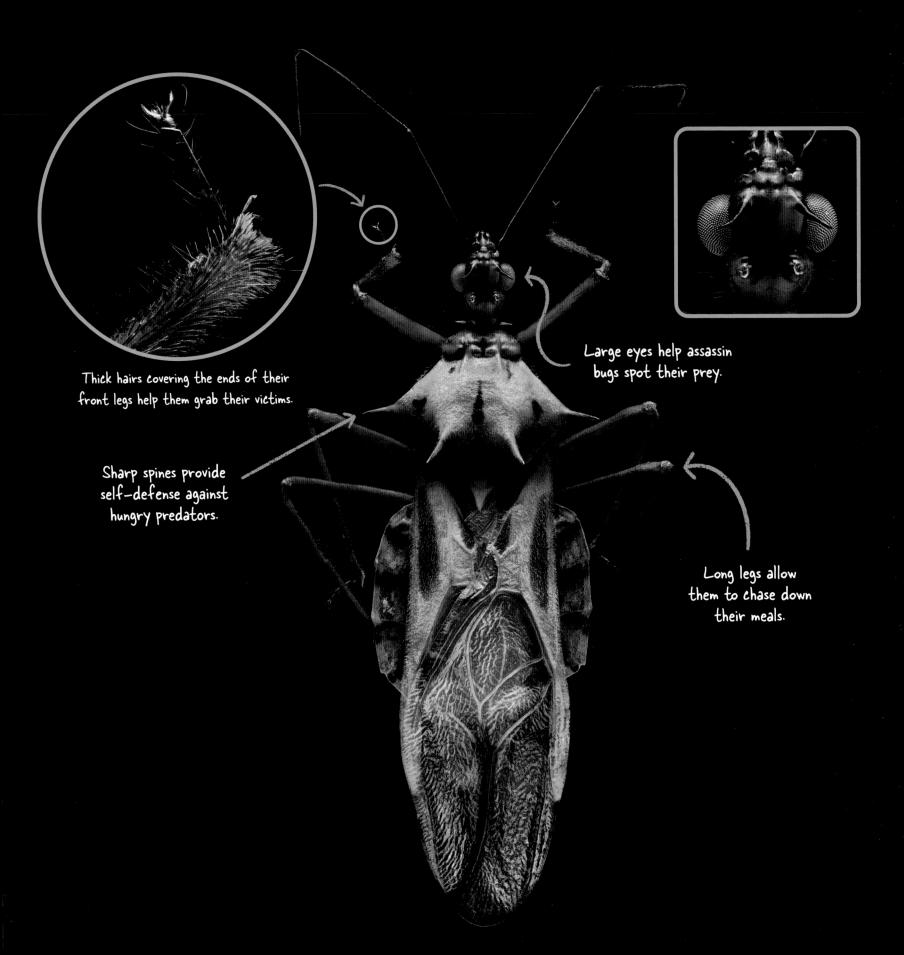

Thick hairs covering the ends of their front legs help them grab their victims.

Large eyes help assassin bugs spot their prey.

Sharp spines provide self-defense against hungry predators.

Long legs allow them to chase down their meals.

ASSASSIN BUG
BOLIVIA ▪ 20 MM LONG

This bug is brutal. It grabs bees and other prey with its front legs, stabs them with a needle-like body part called a **rostrum**, then pumps them full of saliva. But this isn't a normal stream of spit. The assassin bug's saliva turns its victim's insides into goo. Then the insect uses its rostrum like a straw, sucking up its meal.

FACTS

→ Some assassin bugs rub their hairy legs against plants to pick up the pretty smell. Bees are attracted to this scent, but once they get close, the bug grips them tight. A stab, some spit, and no more buzzing for the bee.

→ Assassin bugs steal snacks from other creatures too. They creep across spiderwebs to feast on trapped insects.

→ Some assassin bugs stick dirt or dead insects onto their backs to hide. Scientists call these coverings **backpacks**. But you wouldn't want to stick your homework into one of them; your teacher might not appreciate the grime smeared across your math worksheet.

→ In some parts of the world, these creatures bite you on your lips while you're sleeping, so they're known as kissing bugs. But you don't want a kiss from an assassin bug. Or any bug. Don't kiss an alien either. Or a gorilla.

TIGER BEETLE

BORNEO • 10 MM LONG

For its size, the tiger beetle is one of the fastest creatures on Earth. If these tiny insects were as big as people, they'd run ten times faster than the speediest human alive. They eat anything they can catch, including other beetles, and they run so quickly that they actually go blind briefly. Luckily, they have a few tricks that help them snag food even when they can't see.

FACTS

→ Tiger beetles have very sharp vision. Once a beetle eyes a possible victim, it starts to sprint.

→ The beetle runs so fast that its brain cannot make sense of the light flooding its eyes, so the creature goes blind. To prevent itself from crashing into a rock, the beetle lowers its long, thin antennae out in front as it sprints.

→ If the antennae hit something, the beetle either hurdles or grabs the object.

→ The blindness is brief. Sometimes the beetle stops until it can see again. Then it tracks its prey and dashes ahead. A beetle may stop and start three or four times before catching its meal. Imagine if you were its prey? Just when you think the hunter has given up and you'll live to crawl another day, it starts charging forward again. Bummer.

→ If a tiger beetle accidentally runs over its victim while blind, sensitive hairs on its legs help it feel the prey. Then the bug stops and backs up.

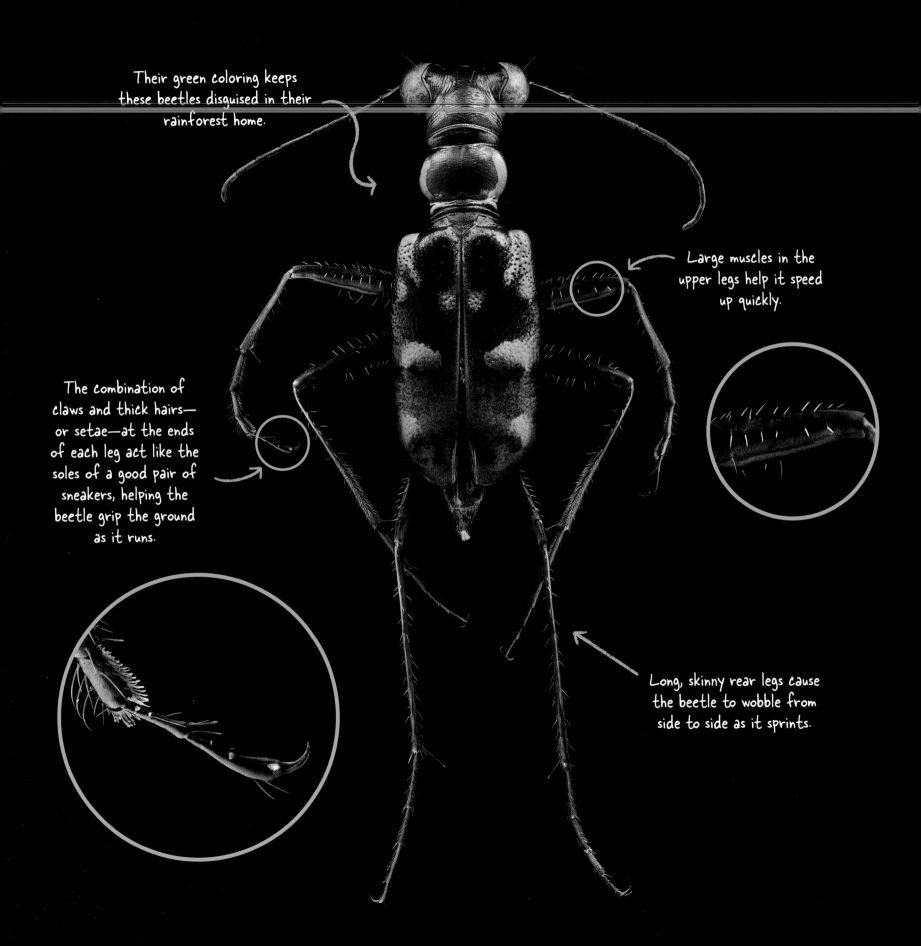

Their green coloring keeps these beetles disguised in their rainforest home.

Large muscles in the upper legs help it speed up quickly.

The combination of claws and thick hairs— or setae—at the ends of each leg act like the soles of a good pair of sneakers, helping the beetle grip the ground as it runs.

Long, skinny rear legs cause the beetle to wobble from side to side as it sprints.

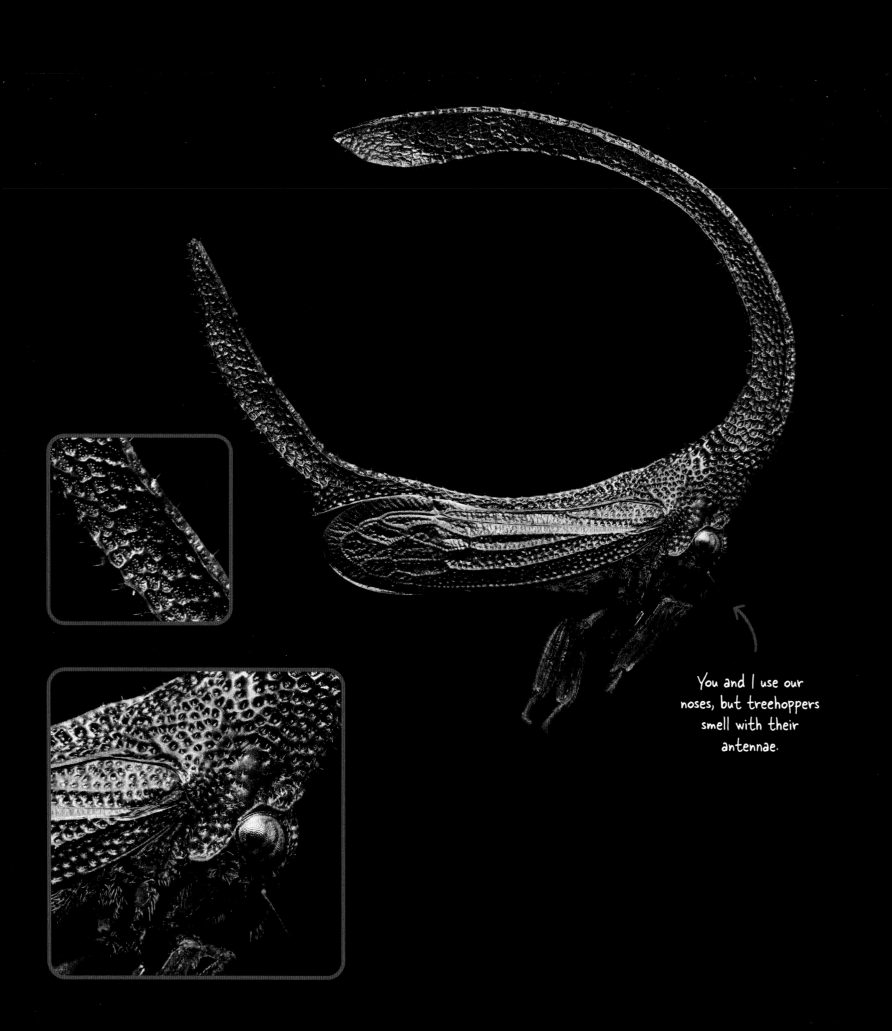

You and I use our noses, but treehoppers smell with their antennae.

BRANCH-BACKED TREEHOPPER

BELIZE ▪ 12 MM LONG

Sure, it might win an award at a fashion show, but the strange helmet curving off the back of this insect is not a fancy hat. It actually helps treehoppers like this one hide. These creatures are great jumpers, too, thanks to the thick muscles in their legs. They push with their rear legs, catapulting off the ground. When a treehopper jumps, you can often hear a slight click.

FACTS

→ Although they can jump, treehoppers spend more time sitting around. They latch onto trees and drink up the sugary sap.

→ When treehoppers are filled up with tree sap and have to, um, relieve themselves, they release a sugary liquid called **honeydew**. Ants love this honeydew so much that they'll protect the treehoppers from other predators. All so they can drink down that delicious honeydew. Which is actually . . . Okay, never mind. You get it, right?

→ Dense hairs around the insect's head and in the dimples on its wings probably* help it sense air movement.

→ What if you had antennae instead of a nose? You'd have to throw away all your sunglasses because they'd fall off your face. But you wouldn't need the nose hair clippers you keep in your school desk either.

→ A tiny hair hides in the center of each dimple along the treehopper's wings and helmet. These hairs may help the creatures feel wind currents.

→ Some treehopper helmets have sharp spikes to keep away predators. You wouldn't take a bite of a cheeseburger if it had spikes sticking out of the top, would you? Wait, you would? Someone feed this kid, please.

*"Probably"? Why probably? Well, scientists don't always know exactly how each part of an insect's body is used or how it might benefit the creature. So they study the feature, observe the insect, and combine their findings with what they know about the subject to make an educated or informed guess.

THE SCIENCE OF BUGS

Maybe you've stomped on an ant before. Or swatted a fly. The scientists who study insects—known as **entomologists**—would ask you to reconsider killing these miniature wonders the next time you spot one. Instead of smooshing that ant, study the little creature. See where it goes and whether other ants follow.

Ask yourself what it's doing and why.

After all, insects are a very, very big part of our planet. They chew up and break down dead and rotting trees and animals and help turn the waste back into soil. Insects pollinate flowering plants, too, and without them, we humans might not survive.

There are more insects than humans—and more *kinds* of insects too. Humans are what we call a species, or a particular type of life. Entomologists and other researchers have already discovered more than 1,000,000 different species of insects. Think about that. One type of person. A million different types of insects!

That includes more than 400,000 species of beetles.

More than 20,000 types of bees.

There are even 12,000 different types of ants.

And this is just what we've found so far!

Some scientists say that if you were to dig through your own backyard and you had the tools to search closely, you'd probably find a new species of insect right there in the dirt. So why not start now? There's nothing preventing you from becoming an entomologist today. Head outside, drop to the dirt, and start searching. You just might find something marvelous.

Strong, clawed front legs help these beetles dig tunnels.

With the help of their hairy hind legs, they drag and push animal droppings and meat into the tunnels. Then they carefully place their eggs on these little meals. When their babies, or larvae, finally hatch, they have food already waiting for them.

SPLENDID-NECKED DUNG BEETLE

MADAGASCAR ▪ 10 MM LONG

Splendid-necked dung beetles don't just eat dung. I mean, sure, they love poo. But there's more to their diet. On the island of Madagascar, where the insect photographed here was discovered, scientists believe that these beetles survived by switching their diet from animal droppings to meat. Not just any meat, though. They feed on carrion, or the rotting flesh of dead animals. Yum.

FACTS

→ Dung beetles can fly long distances in search of . . . yes, you guessed it: dung.

→ A second set of wings—the **elytra**—protect the more delicate flight wings.

→ The splendid-necked dung beetle has small eyes, but its powerful antennae detect the delightful smells of fresh dung and rotting meat far away. Alert! Festering flesh ahead!

→ Dung beetles can also fold in the tips of their antennae for protection against attackers.

→ Most insect parents leave their kids to figure out how to survive on their own. But some dung beetle moms and dads actually tend to the balls of dung or rotting meat, scraping off mold so the food stays fresh. They also guard the entrance to the larvae's burrow to protect the little ones.

→ Scientists once found 16,000 dung beetles in a large pile of elephant poop. They'd flown in from all over. Talk about a party.

→ All that swarming around poo is really, really important. If not for dung beetles, many farms might be smothered by cow droppings. By eating the dung and helping to turn it into soil, dung beetles save American farmers hundreds of millions of dollars each year.

MANTIS-FLY

FRANCE • 14 MM LONG

The mantis-fly might look like a praying mantis, but the two aren't actually related. When some types of mantis-flies are in their larval stage, which is kind of like elementary school, they sneak into the egg sacs of spiders. Once inside, they suck the yolk out of the eggs through a straw-like tongue, deflating them like old soccer balls. A young mantis-fly might also spend a whole winter attached to an adult spider, drinking its blood to stay alive, then climb down once it has spun its egg sac and feast away. What a wonderful guest.

FACTS

→ Most insects use all six legs to walk. The mantis-fly only uses four and saves its forelegs to grasp and hold its prey. When it walks, the mantis-fly tucks these claws under its body.

→ Mantis-flies have two sets of wings, but these little monsters are not great fliers as adults.

→ Antennae help males sniff out females. But tracking down a lady fly isn't always the best plan. Sometimes female mantis-flies will eat the dudes. The guys have eaten the girls too. Either way, not a great first date.

→ They'll munch on anything they can grab with their claw-like forelegs, including fruit flies and other insects.

→ The size of an adult mantis-fly depends on how many spider eggs it can devour in its larval stage. The more eggs, the bigger the adult. That doesn't really apply to humans, but unless you're vegan, you should eat eggs too. Regular ones. Not from spiders.

→ Even though they eat a ton as larvae, young mantis-flies can't poop. They just hold it in, like a little kid on a school field trip, because their stomachs aren't fully developed yet. Only this field trip lasts about a year. Their first act as adults? Going to the bathroom, fly-style.

→ Female mantis-flies lay anywhere from a few hundred to several thousand eggs. Can you imagine having a thousand siblings? You'd never get the good seat in the car, and you'd always be waiting for someone to get out of the bathroom.

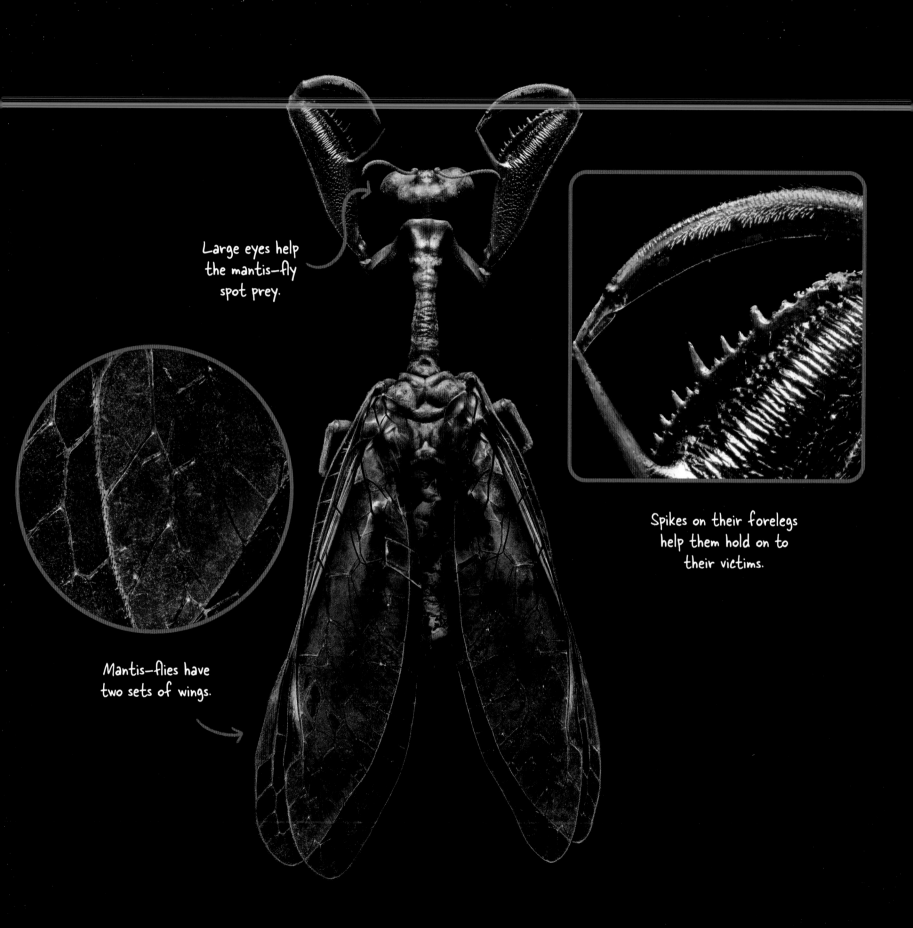

Large eyes help
the mantis-fly
spot prey.

Spikes on their forelegs
help them hold on to
their victims.

Mantis-flies have
two sets of wings.

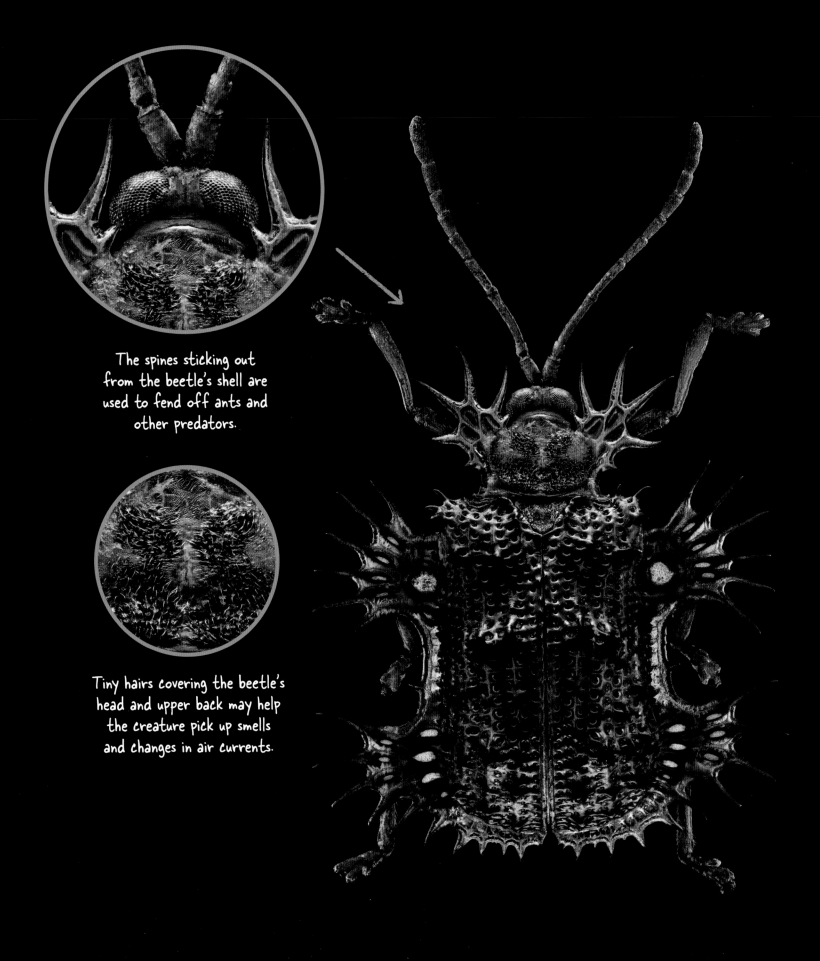

The spines sticking out from the beetle's shell are used to fend off ants and other predators.

Tiny hairs covering the beetle's head and upper back may help the creature pick up smells and changes in air currents.

TORTOISE BEETLE

CHINA ▪ 7 MM LONG

These armored insects are called tortoise beetles because their dome-shaped, dimpled backs look a little like tortoise shells . . . if you crossed them with ancient samurai warriors. They belong to the leaf beetle family, and as they move over the surface of a tasty snack, they resemble miniature armored tanks.

FACTS

→ The many spines sticking out from the beetle's shell are most likely used to fend off ants and other predators. They could also help the beetles hide.

→ Tiny hairs covering the beetle's head and upper back may help the creature pick up smells and changes in air currents.

→ Beneath its armored wing cases, the tortoise beetle hides more delicate wings used for flight.

→ As larvae, tortoise beetles are very vulnerable because they have no protective covering, but they have developed a very unusual self-defense trick. Leaf beetles, such as the tortoise beetle, don't poop and run. They extend part of their butt and drop off their business on top of their shells. This creates a shield above their backs, almost like an umbrella, made out of their droppings. Disgusting? Sure. But these shields help the creatures survive long enough to grow into armored adults.

DARKLING BEETLE

NAMIBIA ▪ 6 MM LONG

This creature gets its name because of how it seeks out and hides in dark, cool places to escape the daytime heat. Darkling beetles are also very good at saving and storing up the water they drink, which helps them survive in the desert. So they're kind of like camels. Actually, they're not like camels. Not at all. Who told you that? They're beetles.

FACTS

→ Some darkling beetles talk to one another through drumming: They strike their **abdomen**, or the end part of their body, down against the ground repeatedly. This creates a knocking sound. Other beetles in the area can guess the direction of the drummer.

→ Many desert darkling beetles act like miniature six-legged skunks and spray stinky chemicals at predators.

→ In one type of darkling beetle, this foul-smelling substance trickles through a gutter below the outer edge of the creature's protective elytra. At first, they can crank out one of these defensive stinks every few minutes, but then they need four or five days to build up their supply of stench again.

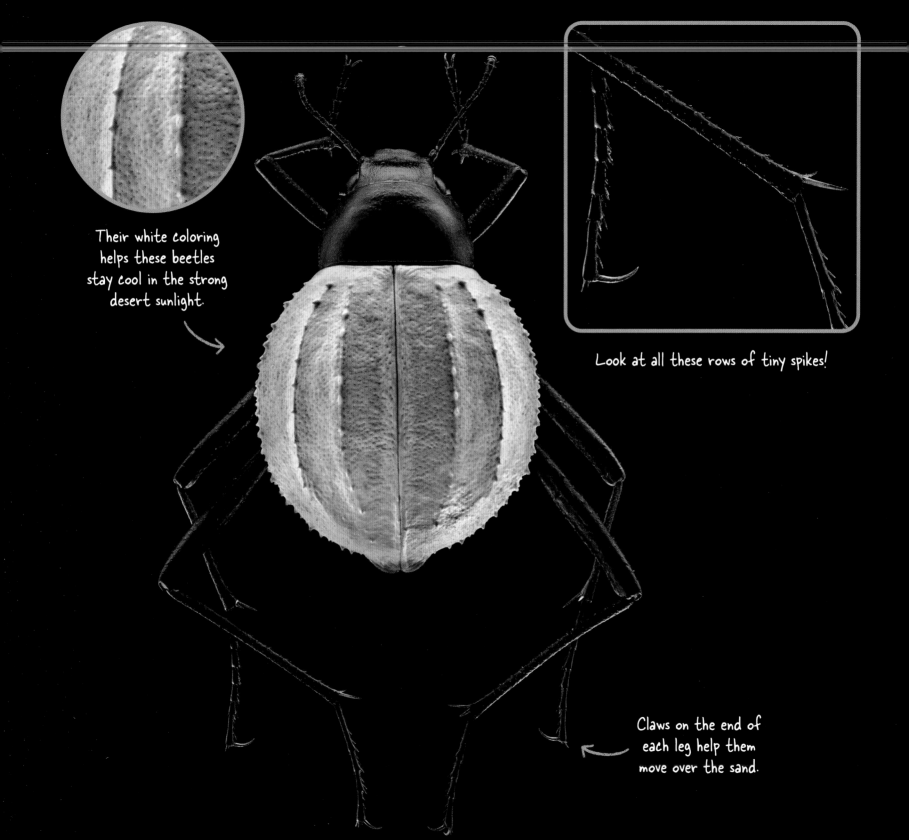

Their white coloring
helps these beetles
stay cool in the strong
desert sunlight.

Look at all these rows of tiny spikes!

Claws on the end of
each leg help them
move over the sand.

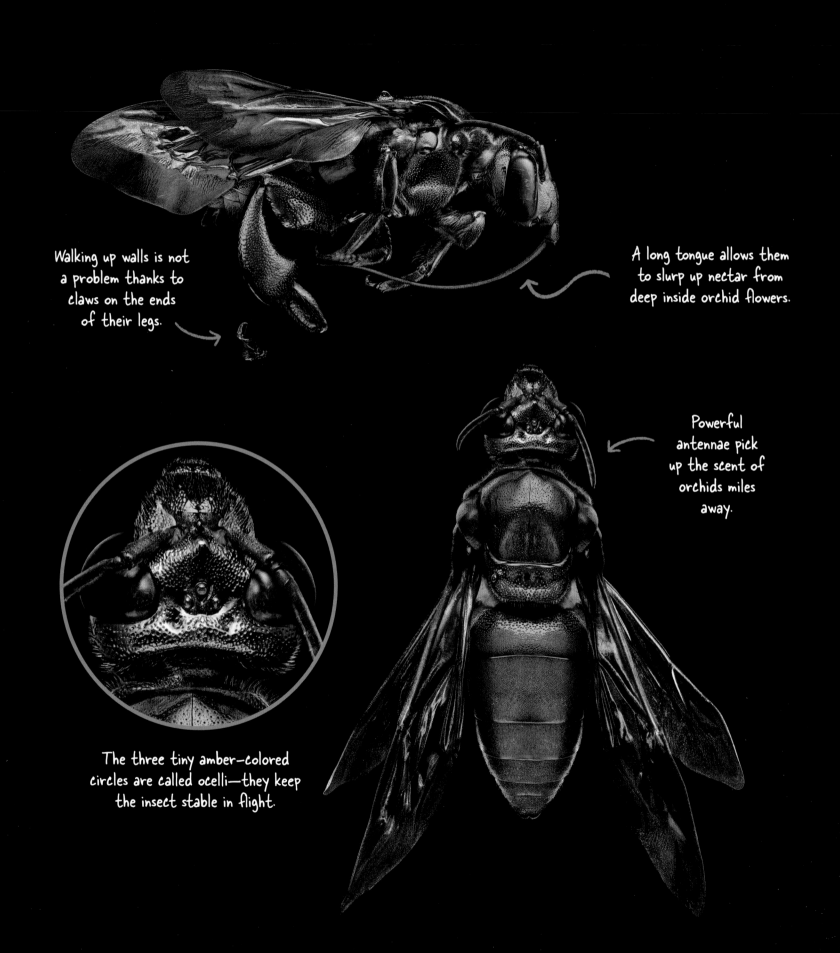

Walking up walls is not a problem thanks to claws on the ends of their legs.

A long tongue allows them to slurp up nectar from deep inside orchid flowers.

Powerful antennae pick up the scent of orchids miles away.

The three tiny amber-colored circles are called ocelli—they keep the insect stable in flight.

ORCHID CUCKOO BEE

BRAZIL • 16 MM LONG

Most bees stock their own nests with pollen as food for their kids. The orchid cuckoo bee lets others do all the work. Females search for the nests of other bees. When they find one that has been stocked with tasty pollen, they lay their eggs right inside with the eggs of the other bee. These little ones are not very good roommates, though. Once an orchid cuckoo bee egg hatches, the larva munches up all the other eggs. If you were a bug, you definitely wouldn't want to invite one of them to a sleepover.

Male orchid cuckoo bees are also perfume collectors with an incredible set of tools to help them find, store, and spread flowery scents. Their goal? To attract ladies. People put on fancy clothes and makeup to get dates. Orchid cuckoo bees use a natural perfume.

FACTS

→ Once a male finds a flower, it spits a kind of grease onto the smelly surface, then uses its hairy forelegs to mop up the scent.

→ The bee uses its middle legs to brush the scent off its front legs, clearing them for the next collection.

→ Inside its large hind legs, the orchid cuckoo bee has a storage pouch. The middle legs transfer the flowery smells here.

→ Once the pouches in its hind legs are full, the male reaches back and covers its middle legs with the perfume.

→ As it flies, the bee brushes its middle legs against small combs at the base of its wings, releasing the attractive smell into the air. All to find a girlfriend!

→ To get both pairs of wings moving together, a row of Velcro-like hairs along the tops of each set of wings latches them onto one another.

POTTER WASP

INDIA ▪ 1.8 CM LONG

The potter wasp (no relation to the family of wizards) earned its name because of its unusual nests. These solitary insects gather sand, soil, and mud to build nests that look like clay pots. The female potter wasp tracks down caterpillars, paralyzes them with her sting, and drops them into the nest. After she packs in about a dozen of these snacks, she deposits her egg, sometimes letting it hang from a thin thread, then seals the top of the nest with more mud. Weeks later, when the egg hatches, her larva has plenty to eat.

FACTS

→ Potter wasps have a very strong sense of smell.

→ In potter wasp families, dads are sort of useless. They don't help with the nests or collect the food or even make the cool little threads that hold the eggs. If they were human dads, they'd probably just sit around watching football and belching.

→ Informed gardeners don't mind seeing a potter wasp's nest near their vegetables because it means something is eating the caterpillars that chew up so many leaves.

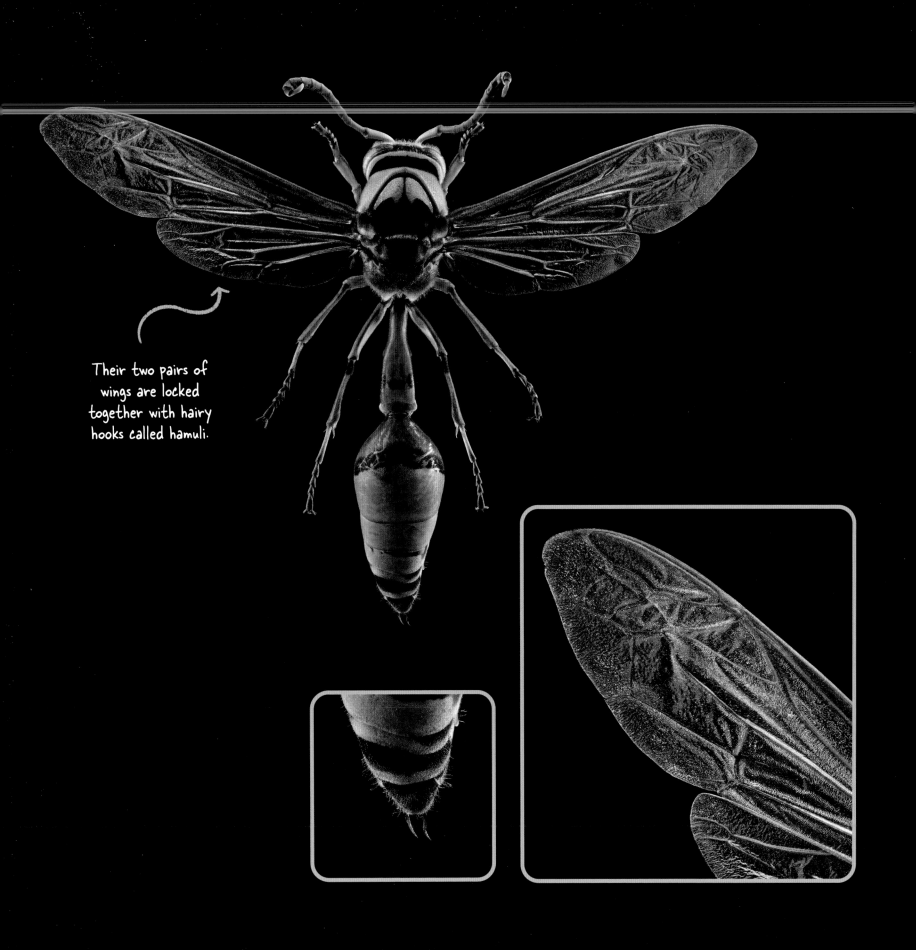

Their two pairs of wings are locked together with hairy hooks called hamuli.

The ruby-tailed wasp has a very hard outer layer, or **cuticle**, that protects it against stings from other wasps.

RUBY-TAILED WASP

FRANCE ▪ 6 MM LONG

This creature might not look frightening, but the ruby-tailed wasp does have some amazing ways of defending itself. These tricks are helpful because this insect acts like a cuckoo bee and sneaks into the nests of other creatures to drop off its eggs. Sometimes the female wasp gets caught inside when the real mother comes to check on her brood.

FACTS

→ A female ruby-tailed wasp lays her eggs in the nest of another female wasp or bee. When those larvae hatch, they eat the eggs belonging to the original mother.

→ Sometimes the host mother returns home to the nest while the ruby-tailed wasp is still inside. If the host wasp finds this invader, she stings.

→ To defend itself, the ruby-tailed wasp can tuck its vulnerable antennae and legs underneath its body, then curl up into a ball like an armadillo. Bites and stings from the host don't harm the wasp because of that tough outer layer.

→ Wasps have different scents, so the host mother can smell an intruder. But some cuckoo wasps have found a way to copy the scent of the host. This way, they can hide in the nest even when the mother arrives home.

THE STRANGE WORLD OF SETAE

Insect expert Stanislav Gorb says the beautiful close-up images in this book only begin to reveal the fabulous details of these creatures. Gorb and other scientists use special instruments to view the tiny setae, or hair-like bits, sticking out of the insects. "It's a whole universe down there," he says. "These setae are not just decoration. They have a purpose." Some help insects stick to surfaces or sense movement in the air around them. Other types help them stay warm during the cold winter. The setae of some beetles prevent dung from sticking to their backs. In blowflies, tiny setae prevent their wings from sticking together in the morning when they're covered in dew. Insects might not have noses or ears or skin like you and I do, but these setae, along with other sensory tools, help them feel, touch, hear, and smell the world around them in amazing ways.

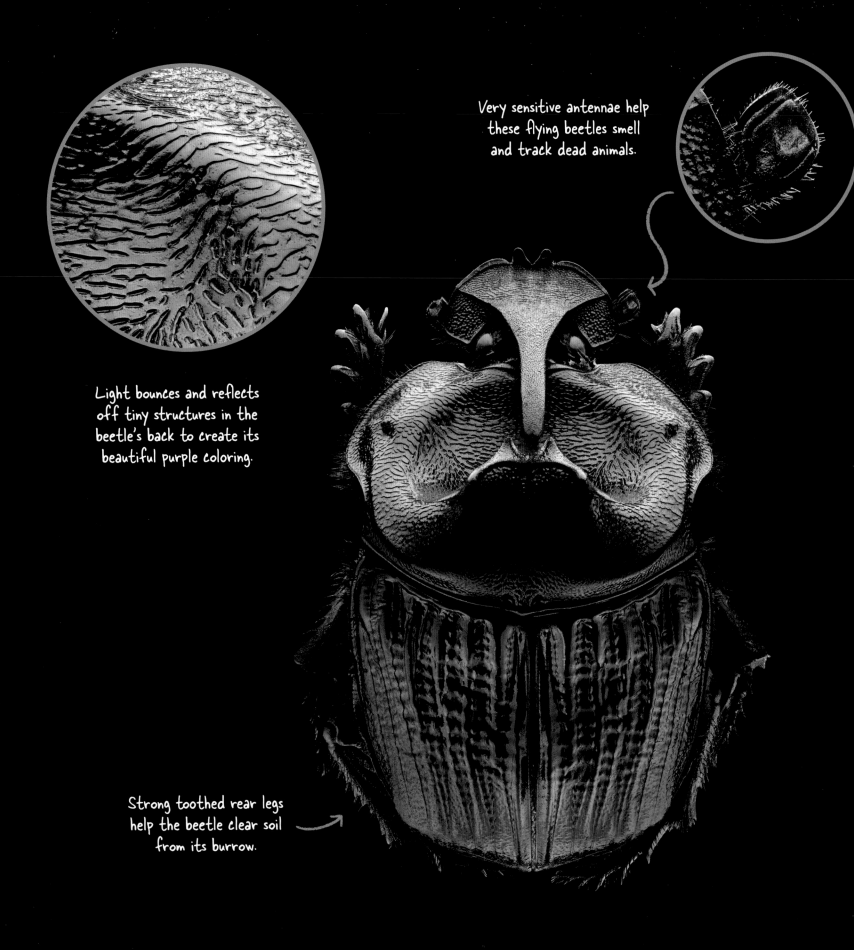

Very sensitive antennae help these flying beetles smell and track dead animals.

Light bounces and reflects off tiny structures in the beetle's back to create its beautiful purple coloring.

Strong toothed rear legs help the beetle clear soil from its burrow.

AMAZONIAN PURPLE WARRIOR SCARAB

PERU ▪ 5 CM LONG

These large scarab beetles are found in the area of the rain forest surrounding the famous Amazon River. Scarab beetles have an amazing history. The ancient Egyptians believed scarab beetles were related to the famous sun god Ra. Like the splendid-necked dung beetle, Amazonian purple warrior scarabs prefer to eat rotting meat instead of animal droppings. Really, though, who wouldn't?

FACTS

→ They are **crepuscular**, which means they're most active at sunrise and sunset. Little kids can be crepuscular too. They get up too early, then they won't go to bed when it's time to settle down. But they don't eat rotting meat. Or most of them don't, anyway.

→ The Amazon purple warrior scarab is very noisy when it flies.

→ The front legs and toothed blades near the head probably help the beetle carve off strips of meat.

→ The warrior scarab's horn helps it grip other beetles in battle or pry another insect off a piece of food. Hey, good rotting meat is hard to find. You need to fight for it.

→ When these beetles find a dead animal, they dig tunnels under the carcass. Then they tear off pieces of meat and drop them into these tunnels, or **burrows**. Inside, they shape them into lumps, or meatballs, which are not at all like your grandmother's meatballs. The female drops an egg on top of each morsel so the larva has something to eat when it hatches.

→ Similar to dung beetles, males will guard the entrance to a burrow and use their horns to keep other beetles away. Nobody's going to mess with those meatballs. Nobody!

PLEASING FUNGUS BEETLE

BOLIVIA ▪ 8 MM LONG

The pleasing fungus beetle is a close relative of the ladybug, and it does not have a pleasing smell. Scientists think these bugs may release either a nasty odor or a stinky substance when attacked. The beautiful colors might be appealing to humans, but they signal predators to stay away.

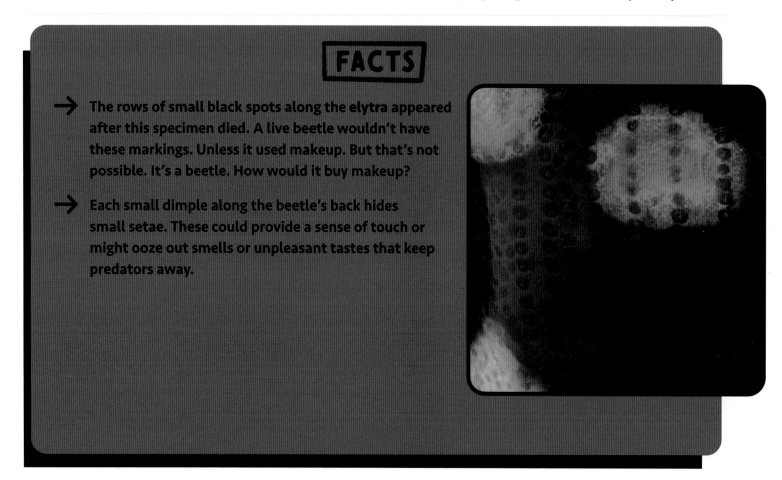

FACTS

→ The rows of small black spots along the elytra appeared after this specimen died. A live beetle wouldn't have these markings. Unless it used makeup. But that's not possible. It's a beetle. How would it buy makeup?

→ Each small dimple along the beetle's back hides small setae. These could provide a sense of touch or might ooze out smells or unpleasant tastes that keep predators away.

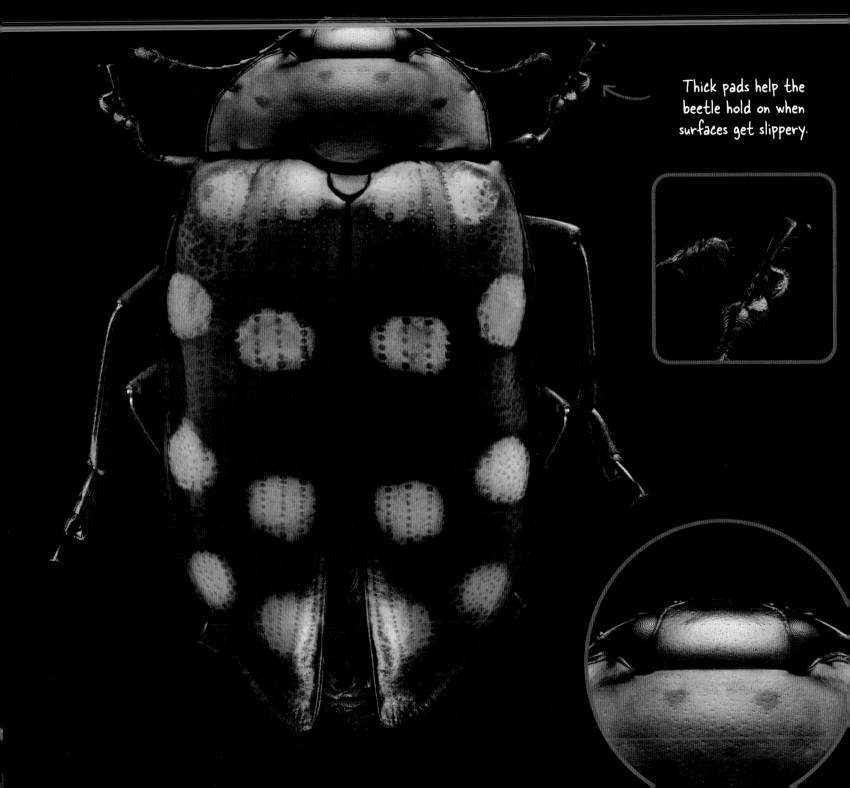

Thick pads help the
beetle hold on when
surfaces get slippery.

Jewel beetles are fast fliers
and swift runners.

The wings of this jewel beetle are hidden
below its protective—and beautiful—elytra.

TRICOLORED JEWEL BEETLE

INDONESIA ▪ 12–16 MM LONG

These beautiful beetles are so tough as larvae that they can chew through wood. In some parts of the world, people used to think that eating them would make you more attractive. Unless people actually saw you eating the beetle. Luckily, scientists prefer to study these creatures, not munch on them. When the famous explorer Alfred Russel Wallace spent four years traveling a group of islands in Southeast Asia called the Malay Archipelago, he collected more than a thousand types of beetles. He declared the tricolored jewel beetle photographed here to be one of the best-looking of its kind.

FACTS

→ Adults eat both leaves and flowers.

→ Tough outer shells protect them against predators.

→ Tiny grooves in their forelegs help them clean their antennae and heads. Imagine if you had those? It would be as if you had a hairbrush permanently stuck in one elbow and a toothbrush in the other. Sure, it would be strange, and hard to pull on a sweatshirt. But you'd always have a way to fix your hair, and no one could ever steal your toothbrush at a sleepover.

→ Jewel beetles lay eggs in dead or dying trees. When the eggs hatch, the larvae chew their way through the wood, forming tiny tunnels.

→ Some jewel beetles can sense forest fires burning miles away. They race to the site of the fires to lay their eggs in fallen trees. After they stop burning, of course.

→ Scientists have found 15,000 different species of jewel beetles.

IRIDESCENT BARK MANTIS

SUMATRA ▪ 4 CM LONG

These beautiful creatures can be found in Southeast Asia, mostly in Sumatra, Indonesia, and India. They hang out under the loose bark of trees or on leaves, then dash after their prey when they spot a tasty morsel. Sometimes they can be picky, though. Back in the early twentieth century, when the naturalist Charles Shelford studied these insects, he found that the iridescent bark mantis he'd captured had no interest in butterflies, termites, or flies. After he offered the mantis a cockroach, however, the little insect quickly attacked the bug with its spiny forelegs and gobbled it up.

FACTS

→ The iridescent bark mantis doesn't sit around waiting for its food to arrive like a grown-up who just ordered takeout. These insects actively chase down their prey.

→ Large eyes help the bark mantis see all around—in front, to the sides, and almost right behind. Imagine if your teachers had eyes like that? You'd never get away with anything. They'd be giant insects, though, so you'd probably behave anyway.

→ The iridescent bark mantis has two sets of wings, but no protective **elytra**.

→ Some scientists think the mantis uses the longer spike on its forelegs to pry its victims out of their hiding spots before grabbing them. Another expert suggests that the insects might use it to spear prey.

→ The iridescent bark mantis doesn't just like to eat cockroaches. It also runs like them, with its body low to the ground.

→ When it's not chasing or devouring prey, the iridescent bark mantis can fold its ferocious forelegs under its body.

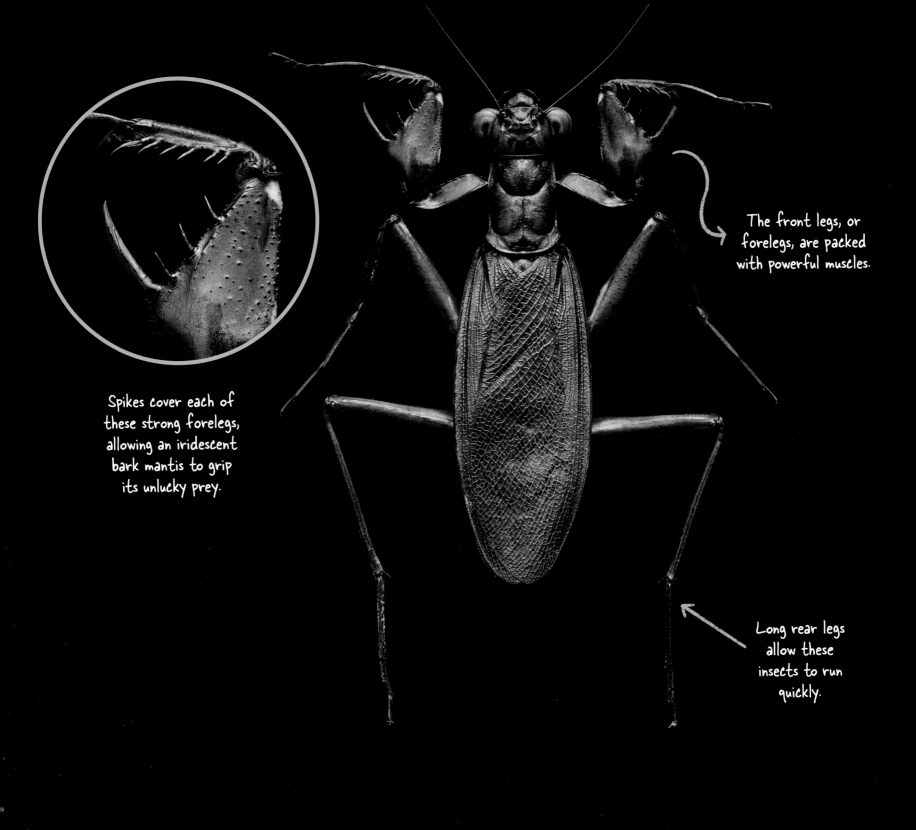

Spikes cover each of these strong forelegs, allowing an iridescent bark mantis to grip its unlucky prey.

The front legs, or forelegs, are packed with powerful muscles.

Long rear legs allow these insects to run quickly.

GLOSSARY

ANTENNAE: Our cars and phones have antennae to pick up radio and phone signals. Insects use their antennae for all kinds of things, including smell!

BEETLE: An insect with a hard outer set of wings that protects the more delicate wings below.

BUG: This is actually a tricky word, according to entomologist James Hogan. Sometimes people use it to talk about any insect-like creature, as we've done in the book. But it also refers to insects that typically have a straw-like mouth that allows them to suck up juice from plants or the gooey insides of their victims.

CREPUSCULAR: When creatures are more active at dawn, when the sun is rising, and again at dusk, when it is setting, they are crepuscular. (Writers can be like that too.)

CRYPSIS: This is a strategy insects use either to avoid predators or catch prey. It's all about hiding, either by using camouflage, burrowing into the ground, or blending into the background.

ELYTRA: Protective wings that cover the more fragile wings used for flying.

ENTOMOLOGY: The study of insects!

EXOSKELETON: A kind of shell that supports the insect's body, in the same way bones hold up humans. Iron Man wears an exoskeleton too. But even with all his lasers and blasters, I'm not sure he'd beat a giant assassin bug.

FORELEGS: Insects don't have arms. Even when those not-arms are used for grabbing prey and not for walking, as in the mantis-fly, they're still called forelegs. Weird, right?

LARVAE: The insect version of a kid. Imagine, though, if you weren't just a smaller version of an adult, but weirdly monstrous. That's more like a larva. Some insects, like the Marion flightless moth, spend more time as larvae than they do as adults. Humans can be like that too, when they refuse to grow up and move out of their parents' house.

MANDIBLES: Almost like miniature claws, the mandibles are part of the mouths of some insects, and they're used to hold, crush, or chew food.

SETAE: These are the tiny hair-like structures you see all over the insects Levon has photographed. But they're not like hairs at all. Some can sense the direction of the wind. Others help spread sticky fluids.

SCOPAE: Miniature brooms or brushes used to transport pollen.

STRIDULATION: A way that insects talk to one another, by rubbing certain parts of their body together to create a raspy or chirping sound.

LEARN MORE ABOUT THE MARVELOUS WORLD OF MICROSCULPTURE

Normally an author wouldn't send his or her readers to the Internet. Not when there are shelves and shelves stacked with wonderful printed books waiting to be devoured at your local bookstores and libraries. But Levon and a few of his friends built an absolutely amazing website that allows you to zoom in on his images of these insects and really study the details up close. Go to microsculpture.net, find an insect that interests you, and have fun!

SPECIAL THANKS

Thank you to scientists James Hogan, Rob Cannings, Steven Chown, Rex Cocroft, Cole Gilbert, Stanislav Gorb, Santiago Ramírez, Kurt Redborg, Vonnie Shields, Paul Skelley, and Kate Umbers for sharing their time and providing valuable insights. And thank you to entomologist John Capinera and all the contributors to his fabulous treatise, the *Encyclopedia of Entomology*.

With thanks to the Oxford University Museum of Natural History.

ABOUT THE AUTHOR

Gregory Mone is the author or coauthor of ten books for adults and children, including the Jack and the Geniuses series with Bill Nye and the novel *Fish*. He is a contributing editor at *Popular Science* and lives on Martha's Vineyard with his family and many insects. The insects live outside, though, not in the house. Well, mostly. Learn more at gregorymone.com.

ABOUT THE PHOTOGRAPHER

Levon Biss is a British photographer living in the English countryside. For more than twenty years, his work concentrated on people—he has photographed top athletes, presidents, and countless celebrities—but these days his work focuses on the natural world, the microscopic world in particular. His unique photography has been exhibited all around the globe and is held in numerous public and private collections, including the National Museum of Qatar and the American Museum of Natural History. To view more of Levon's work, visit levonbiss.com.